Dear Parent:

Buckle up! You are about to join your child on a very exciting journey. The destination? Independent reading!

Road to Reading will help you and your child get there. The program offers books at five levels, or Miles, that accompany children from their first attempts at reading to successfully reading on their own. Each Mile is paved with engaging stories and delightful artwork.

Getting Started

For children who know the alphabet and are eager to begin reading
- easy words • fun rhythms • big type • picture clues

Reading With Help

For children who recognize some words and sound out others with help
- short sentences • pattern stories • simple plotlines

Reading On Your Own

For children who are ready to read easy stories by themselves
- longer sentences • more complex plotlines • easy dialogue

First Chapter Books

For children who want to take the plunge into chapter books
- bite-size chapters • short paragraphs • full-color art

Chapter Books

For children who are comfortable reading independently
- longer chapters • occasional black-and-white illustrations

There's no need to hurry through the Miles. Road to Reading is designed without age or grade levels. Children can progress at their own speed, developing confidence and pride in their reading ability no matter what their age or grade.

So sit back and enjoy the ride—every Mile of the way!

To Katie
Grow on—and enjoy each
new turn of the road
B.S.H.

To Magnanimous Maggie
D.J.

Library of Congress Cataloging-in-Publication Data
Hazen, Barbara Shook.
Road Hog / by Barbara Shook Hazen ; illustrated by Davy Jones.
　 p.　cm. — (Road to reading.　Mile 2)
Summary:　Road Hog loves to speed and drive recklessly until Police Dog
tows his car.
ISBN 0-307-26201-4 (pbk.)
[1. Pigs—Fiction.　2. Animals—Fiction.　3. Automobile
driving—Fiction.　4. Stories in rhyme.]　I. Jones, Davy, ill.
II. Title.　III. Series.
PZ8.3.H3339　Ro 1998
[E]—dc21

98-12756
CIP
AC

A GOLDEN BOOK • New York
Golden Books Publishing Company, Inc. New York, New York 10106

ISBN: 0-307-26201-4

A MCMXCVIII

Road Hog

by Barbara Shook Hazen
illustrated by Davy Jones

Look out!

Road Hog likes
to go too fast.

Road Hog gives

his horn a blast.

Road Hog cries,
"Fast is fun!"

Road Hog passes
everyone.

He passes Skunk
and Mole and Rat.

10

He passes Cow
and Horse and Cat.

"Look, no hands!"
Road Hog cries.

Can he do it?

Road Hog tries.

He drives to the left.

He drives to the right.

He doesn't see
the traffic light.

"Road Hog, stop!"
his friends all cry.

"Wheee!" he yells
as he speeds by.

Police Dog hollers,
"Where's the fire?"

Road Hog speeds
and tears a tire!

He hits the brake.

His wheel goes pop.

It is too late!
He cannot stop.

CRASH!

SMASH!

Police Dog says,
"Next time go slow."

He gives a ticket
and a tow.

Road Hog in tow
goes *very* slow.

Road Hog says,
"Slow's no fun.
Now I'm passed
by everyone!"

"I'm passed by Mole
and Skunk and Rat.

I'm passed by Cow
and Horse and Cat.
I hate that!"

Road Hog gives
his horn a blast.

Road Hog has
slowed down at last!